T0368701

From Division to Unity:
A Guide to
Healing Church Splits

Dr. Mark A. McConnell

authorHOUSE®

AuthorHouse™
1663 Liberty Drive
Bloomington, IN 47403
www.authorhouse.com
Phone: 833-262-8899

Published by AuthorHouse 02/20/2025

ISBN: 979-8-8230-4398-4 (sc)
ISBN: 979-8-8230-4399-1 (e)

Library of Congress Control Number: 2025903359

Print information available on the last page.

FOREWORD

God knows His church and the particular needs of each individual congregation. As a result, He navigates circumstances and situations to strategically unite pastor and people.

As his book reveals, Dr. Mark A. McConnell has pastored three churches; all newly organized and one he organized. Each church comprised of diversely different people with divergently different needs, possessing one commonality, God's servant, Dr. Mark A. McConnell who led them to a place of peace, unity and stability.

A journey through division, Dr. McConnell's personal testimony, is a must read for pastors, and ministry leaders, regardless of their background or church history. The biblical principles and real life strategies highlighted in this book are invaluable for any church that seeks harmony and momentum in ministry.

Dr. Reginald E. Bachus
Pastor, Friendship Baptist Church
Chicago Illinois

TABLE OF CONTENTS

Introduction: A Journey Through Division ix

Chapter 1: The Root Causes of Division 1

Chapter 2: Recognizing the Warning Signs........... 10

Chapter 3: Handling Conflict Biblically 17

Chapter 4: Healing After a Split........................... 25

Chapter 5: The Role of Leadership....................... 33

Chapter 6: Preventing Church Splits
Before They Happen 41

Chapter 7: Restoring Broken Relationships 49

Chapter 8: Embracing a New Beginning............... 57

Chapter 9: The Power of Reconciliation 64

Chapter 10: Moving Forward with Hope 72

Chapter 11: The Final Word................................... 79

INTRODUCTION

A Journey Through Division

Church splits are among the most painful experiences a congregation can endure. They leave wounds that take years to heal, and they test the faith and perseverance of everyone involved. Over my 35 years in ministry, I have witnessed firsthand the challenges and heartache that come with church splits. Each one has left a deep impression on me, shaping my approach to ministry and my understanding of what it means to lead, heal, and rebuild.

I have pastored three churches, all of which were born out of division:

1. **Southside First Baptist Church in Kansas City,** - A congregation that remained after a split, holding on to their faith and seeking stability amid uncertainty.

2. **Prince of Peace Baptist Church in Peoria, Illinois** - A group that left another church, yearning for a fresh start but carrying the wounds of division with them.

3. **New Cornerstone Baptist Church in Peoria, Illinois** - A church I had the privilege of organizing, formed by those seeking a new beginning after another painful separation.

Each of these churches taught me invaluable lessons about the nature of division, the resilience of God's people, and the redemptive power of His love. My role in these pastorates was clear: to love the people, tend to their spiritual wounds, and put things in order, just as the Apostle Paul instructed Titus to do on the island of Crete (Titus 1:5).

WHY THIS BOOK?

Church splits do not happen in isolation. They are often the result of disagreements, conflicts, or unresolved issues that fester over time. While the causes vary, the outcomes are often the same: hurt, disillusionment, and broken fellowship. However, these painful experiences also provide an opportunity for growth, healing, and reflection on what it means to be the body of Christ.

This book is not just about diagnosing the causes of church splits but about offering a path forward. It is a guide for pastors, leaders, and congregations who are navigating the storm of division. It draws from my personal experiences, biblical principles, and practical strategies to help churches heal, reconcile, and thrive.

THE CALL TO UNITY

Psalm 133:1 reminds us, *"Behold, how good and how pleasant it is for brethren to dwell together in unity!"* Unity is not just an ideal; it is a command from God and a reflection of His nature. My prayer is that this book will inspire churches to embrace the hard work of reconciliation, to prioritize unity, and to reflect the love of Christ in all that they do.

Chapter 1

THE ROOT CAUSES OF DIVISION

Church splits are among the most painful and complex challenges that pastors and congregations face. They leave a lasting impact on the people involved, often creating wounds that are difficult to heal. Understanding the root causes of division is essential for addressing the issue effectively and fostering unity within the body of Christ. In this chapter, we will explore the underlying reasons why church splits occur, supported by biblical insights and practical observations.

THE NATURE OF DIVISION

Division is not a new phenomenon. From the early church to the modern era, disagreements and conflicts have tested the unity of believers. The Apostle Paul addressed divisions in the church of Corinth, writing, *"Now I beseech you, brethren, by the name of our Lord Jesus Christ, that ye all speak the same thing, and that there be no divisions among you; but that ye be perfectly joined together in the same mind and in the same judgment"* (1 Corinthians 1:10). Despite Paul's exhortation, human nature often leads to discord.

Church splits generally stem from one or more of the following root causes: pride and ego, doctrinal disagreements, power struggles, miscommunication, and unresolved conflicts. While these issues may manifest differently in each situation, they often intertwine to create a toxic environment that ultimately fractures the congregation.

1. PRIDE AND EGO

Pride is perhaps the most common root cause of division within the church. It often leads to a spirit of competition and self-promotion, which can undermine the mission of the church. Proverbs 16:18 warns, *"Pride goeth before destruction, and an haughty spirit before a fall."* When individuals prioritize their own desires, recognition, or opinions over the greater good, the unity of the church suffers.

Manifestations of Pride in the Church:

Leadership Conflicts: Pride can cause leaders to clash over vision, authority, or personal agendas.

Instead of working collaboratively, they compete for influence, creating factions within the church.

Resistance to Change: Congregants or leaders who resist change due to personal preferences often hinder the church's progress and unity.

Unwillingness to Admit Fault: Pride prevents individuals from acknowledging their mistakes or seeking reconciliation, allowing conflicts to escalate.

2. DOCTRINAL DISAGREEMENTS

Disputes over theology and doctrine are another major cause of church splits. While differences in interpretation are natural, they become divisive when individuals prioritize their personal convictions over the unity of the body.

Paul warned Timothy about the dangers of straying from sound doctrine, writing, *"For the time will come when they will not endure sound doctrine; but after their own lusts shall they heap to themselves teachers, having itching ears"* (2 Timothy 4:3). Disagreements over non-essential doctrines, in particular, often lead to unnecessary division.

Examples of Doctrinal Conflicts:

Disputes over worship styles, such as traditional versus contemporary music.

Differing views on secondary theological issues, such as eschatology or spiritual gifts.

Conflicts over interpretations of church governance or denominational practices.

3. POWER STRUGGLES

Power struggles frequently arise within churches when individuals or groups seek to assert control. These struggles often stem from a desire for recognition, authority, or influence. James 3:16 reminds us, *"For where envying and strife is, there is confusion and every evil work."*

Signs of Power Struggles in Churches:

Cliques and Factions: When groups within the church form alliances based on personal loyalties, they often create an "us versus them" mentality.

Competing Agendas: Leaders or members who push their own agendas rather than seeking God's will contribute to division.

Control Over Resources: Disputes over the allocation of finances, facilities, or ministries can escalate into larger conflicts.

4. MISCOMMUNICATION AND ASSUMPTIONS

Miscommunication is a subtle yet powerful contributor to church splits. When information is misunderstood or withheld, it creates confusion and mistrust. Proverbs 15:1 advises, *"A soft answer turneth away wrath: but grievous words stir up anger."* Clear, honest communication is essential for maintaining unity.

Examples of Miscommunication in Churches:

Leaders failing to explain decisions or changes clearly to the congregation.

Members making assumptions about others' intentions without seeking clarification.

Gossip or rumors spreading misinformation and creating conflict.

5. Unresolved Conflicts

Conflict is inevitable in any community, but unresolved disputes can fester and grow, leading to division. Matthew 18:15-17 provides a clear process for addressing conflicts within the church: *"Moreover if thy brother shall trespass against thee, go and tell him his fault between thee and him alone: if he shall hear thee, thou hast gained thy brother."*

Reasons Why Conflicts Remain Unresolved:

Avoidance of difficult conversations.

Lack of a structured process for conflict resolution.

Bitterness and unforgiveness preventing reconciliation.

Biblical Principles for Addressing Division

The Bible provides guidance for dealing with division and promoting unity within the church. These principles can help leaders and congregations address the root causes of division and prevent splits.

1. **Promote Humility:** Philippians 2:3-4 teaches, *"Let nothing be done through strife or vainglory; but in lowliness of mind let each esteem*

other better than themselves. Look not every man on his own things, but every man also on the things of others." Humility fosters a spirit of cooperation and selflessness.

2. **Encourage Forgiveness:** Ephesians 4:31-32 instructs believers to *"Let all bitterness, and wrath, and anger, and clamour, and evil speaking, be put away from you, with all malice: And be ye kind one to another, tenderhearted, forgiving one another, even as God for Christ's sake hath forgiven you."* Forgiveness is essential for reconciliation and healing.

3. **Prioritize Unity:** Psalm 133:1 declares, *"Behold, how good and how pleasant it is for brethren to dwell together in unity!"* Unity should be a central goal of every congregation.

4. **Address Conflicts Biblically:** Following the steps outlined in Matthew 18:15-17 can prevent misunderstandings from escalating.

5. **Focus on Christ:** Colossians 1:18 reminds us that Christ is the head of the church. Keeping Christ at the center ensures that decisions and actions align with His will.

PRACTICAL STEPS FOR PREVENTING DIVISION

To address and prevent division, churches can take the following proactive measures:

1. **Foster Open Communication:** Regularly share updates, decisions, and vision with the congregation to build trust and transparency.

2. **Provide Conflict Resolution Training:** Equip leaders and members with the tools to handle disputes effectively.

3. **Encourage Servant Leadership:** Promote a culture where leaders serve others rather than seek personal gain.

4. **Focus on Discipleship:** Strengthen the spiritual maturity of the congregation to minimize conflicts rooted in immaturity or misunderstanding.

5. **Celebrate Unity:** Highlight examples of cooperation and harmony within the church to reinforce the value of unity.

CONCLUSION

Church splits are painful, but they are not inevitable. By identifying and addressing the root causes of division, congregations can foster an environment of unity and love. As Paul wrote in Ephesians 4:3, *"Endeavouring to keep the unity of the Spirit in the bond of peace."* Through humility, forgiveness, and a commitment to Christ, the church can overcome the challenges of division and reflect the glory of God to the world.

Chapter 2

RECOGNIZING THE WARNING SIGNS

Church splits rarely happen overnight. Instead, they are often the culmination of unresolved issues, growing tensions, and overlooked warning signs. By recognizing these signs early, church leaders and members can take proactive steps to address potential problems before they escalate into division. In this chapter, we will explore the warning signs of discord within a congregation, drawing from biblical principles and real-life pastoral experiences.

UNDERSTANDING THE EARLY STAGES OF DIVISION

The seeds of division are often sown subtly, through small misunderstandings, unresolved grievances, or unchecked pride. The Apostle Paul wrote to the Corinthians, saying, *"For ye are yet carnal: for whereas there is among you envying, and strife, and divisions, are*

ye not carnal, and walk as men?*" (1 Corinthians 3:3).
This passage highlights that division is a symptom of
spiritual immaturity, often beginning with seemingly
minor issues that are left unaddressed.

In my 35 years of pastoral ministry, I've seen how
ignoring early signs of trouble can lead to major fractures
within a church. At Southside First Baptist Church,
where I pastored a congregation that remained after a
split before my tenure, the signs of discord were evident
long before the separation occurred. Recognizing and
addressing these signs earlier might have prevented
some of the pain that followed.

1. DECLINE IN FELLOWSHIP

A healthy church is marked by strong relationships
and genuine fellowship among its members. When
this begins to decline, it is often an early indicator of
division.

Signs of Declining Fellowship:

Decreased participation in small groups, prayer
meetings, or social gatherings.

Members isolating themselves from others.

A lack of warmth or welcome toward visitors.

The Bible emphasizes the importance of fellowship in Hebrews 10:25, which says, *"Not forsaking the assembling of ourselves together, as the manner of some is; but exhorting one another: and so much the more, as ye see the day approaching."* Restoring fellowship requires intentional efforts to rebuild trust and community.

2. FORMATION OF CLIQUES AND FACTIONS

When small groups within the church begin to form exclusive cliques, it can lead to division. These groups often prioritize their own interests over the unity of the congregation.

Signs of Cliques:

Members forming alliances based on personal preferences or loyalties.

Resistance to new members joining established groups.

Conversations or decisions happening in secret rather than openly.

Paul warned against factions in 1 Corinthians 1:12-13, saying, *"Now this I say, that every one of you saith, I am of Paul; and I of Apollos; and I of Cephas; and I of Christ.*

Is Christ divided?" Unity requires breaking down these barriers and fostering inclusivity.

3. GOSSIP AND NEGATIVE TALK

Gossip and negative speech are often precursors to division. Proverbs 16:28 warns, *"A froward man soweth strife: and a whisperer separateth chief friends."* Unchecked gossip can create mistrust and resentment within the church.

Examples of Negative Talk:

Criticizing church leadership or decisions without offering solutions.

Spreading rumors about other members.

Complaining about changes in worship style, programs, or policies.

4. RESISTANCE TO LEADERSHIP

A growing resistance to leadership is another key warning sign. This can manifest as open defiance or subtle undermining of the pastor's authority.

Signs of Resistance:

Members questioning every decision made by leadership.

Lack of support for church initiatives or programs.

Conversations that challenge leadership outside of proper channels.

Hebrews 13:17 instructs believers, *"Obey them that have the rule over you, and submit yourselves: for they watch for your souls, as they that must give account, that they may do it with joy, and not with grief: for that is unprofitable for you."* Addressing this requires leaders to model humility and engage openly with the congregation.

5. DECLINING SPIRITUAL HEALTH

Spiritual stagnation often precedes division. When members or leaders neglect their spiritual growth, it weakens the overall health of the church.

Indicators of Declining Spiritual Health:

Decreased attendance at worship services and Bible studies.

A lack of personal prayer and devotion among members.

Focus shifting from spiritual growth to personal preferences or conflicts.

Revelation 2:4-5 provides a sobering reminder: *"Nevertheless I have somewhat against thee, because thou hast left thy first love. Remember therefore from whence thou art fallen, and repent, and do the first works."* Restoring spiritual health involves renewing a focus on Christ and His mission.

PRACTICAL STEPS TO ADDRESS WARNING SIGNS

Addressing the warning signs of division requires intentionality and grace. Here are practical steps churches can take:

1. **Foster Open Communication:** Encourage honest, respectful conversations among members and leaders. James 1:19 advises, *"Wherefore, my beloved brethren, let every man be swift to hear, slow to speak, slow to wrath."*

2. **Promote Inclusivity:** Break down cliques by creating opportunities for members to interact and serve together.

3. **Encourage Reconciliation:** Address grievances directly and biblically, following Matthew 18:15-17.

4. **Invest in Discipleship:** Strengthen the spiritual health of the congregation through teaching, mentoring, and prayer.

5. **Support Leadership:** Pray for church leaders and encourage them in their roles.

CONCLUSION

Recognizing the warning signs of division is the first step toward preventing church splits. By addressing these signs early and proactively, churches can foster unity and strengthen their witness to the world. As Paul wrote in Ephesians 4:3, *"Endeavouring to keep the unity of the Spirit in the bond of peace."* Unity requires vigilance, humility, and a commitment to Christ-centered relationships.

Chapter 3

HANDLING CONFLICT BIBLICALLY

Conflict is inevitable in any human relationship, and the church is no exception. However, the way we handle conflict can determine whether it leads to division or reconciliation. The Bible provides clear principles for addressing disagreements in a way that honors God, fosters unity, and promotes healing. This chapter explores biblical strategies for resolving conflicts within the church, emphasizing the importance of humility, communication, and forgiveness.

CONFLICT IS NOT NEW

From the earliest days of the church, conflicts have arisen among believers. In Acts 6:1, we read about a dispute between the Grecians and the Hebrews over the neglect of widows in daily ministration. The apostles addressed this conflict by appointing deacons to oversee the matter, demonstrating the importance of practical solutions rooted in wisdom and fairness. Similarly, Paul and Barnabas experienced a sharp disagreement in Acts 15:36-40, which led to their separation but also to the multiplication of their missionary efforts.

These examples remind us that conflict, when handled biblically, can lead to growth and new opportunities. However, unresolved conflicts can also cause deep wounds and division. As Proverbs 17:14 warns, *"The beginning of strife is as when one letteth out water: therefore leave off contention, before it be meddled with."*

1. ACKNOWLEDGE THE CONFLICT

The first step in handling conflict is to acknowledge its existence. Ignoring or denying conflict often allows it to grow unchecked, leading to greater harm. Jesus taught the importance of addressing conflicts directly in Matthew 5:23-24: *"Therefore if thou bring thy gift to the altar, and there rememberest that thy brother hath ought against thee; Leave there thy gift before the altar, and go thy way; first be reconciled to thy brother, and then come and offer thy gift."*

Practical Steps to Acknowledge Conflict:

Create a culture where concerns can be voiced openly and respectfully.

Encourage leaders to model transparency and humility in addressing issues.

Recognize that conflict is a normal part of relationships and does not signify failure.

2. APPROACH THE CONFLICT WITH HUMILITY

Pride often exacerbates conflict, making it difficult to find resolution. James 4:6 reminds us, *"God resisteth the proud, but giveth grace unto the humble."* Approaching conflict with humility allows all parties to focus on understanding rather than defending their positions.

Biblical Principles for Humility in Conflict:

Examine Yourself First: Before addressing someone else's fault, consider your own contributions to the conflict. Matthew 7:3-5 says, *"And why beholdest thou the mote that is in thy brother's eye, but considerest not the beam that is in thine own eye?"*

Seek God's Guidance: Pray for wisdom and discernment before engaging in difficult conversations.

Listen with an Open Heart: James 1:19 advises, *"Let every man be swift to hear, slow to speak, slow to wrath."*

3. FOLLOW THE BIBLICAL PROCESS FOR RESOLUTION

Jesus outlined a clear process for resolving conflicts within the church in Matthew 18:15-17:

1. **Address the Issue Privately:** *"Moreover if thy brother shall trespass against thee, go and tell him his fault between thee and him alone: if he shall hear thee, thou hast gained thy brother."* Begin by addressing the issue one-on-one to avoid unnecessary embarrassment or escalation.

2. **Involve Witnesses if Necessary:** *"But if he will not hear thee, then take with thee one or two more, that in the mouth of two or three witnesses every word may be established."* Bringing in neutral parties can help provide perspective and accountability.

3. **Bring the Matter Before the Church:** *"And if he shall neglect to hear them, tell it unto the church: but if he neglect to hear the church, let him be unto thee as an heathen man and a publican."* As a last resort, involve the broader church body to seek resolution.

4. PRIORITIZE FORGIVENESS

Forgiveness is central to resolving conflict and restoring relationships. Colossians 3:13 instructs, *"Forbearing one another, and forgiving one another, if any man have a quarrel against any: even as Christ forgave you, so also do ye."* Forgiveness does not mean ignoring wrongdoing but choosing to release bitterness and seek reconciliation.

Steps to Foster Forgiveness:

Acknowledge the hurt and its impact on the relationship.

Choose to let go of resentment, even if the other party does not apologize.

Focus on the example of Christ, who forgave us even while we were yet sinners (Romans 5:8).

5. COMMUNICATE WITH GRACE

Effective communication is essential for resolving conflict. Ephesians 4:29 reminds us, *"Let no corrupt communication proceed out of your mouth, but that which is good to the use of edifying, that it may minister grace unto the hearers."* Words have the power to heal or to harm, so it is vital to speak with grace and truth.

Tips for Graceful Communication:

Speak calmly and respectfully, even in the face of anger or frustration.

Focus on the issue at hand rather than attacking the person.

Use "I" statements to express feelings without assigning blame (e.g., "I felt hurt when..." instead of "You always...").

6. SEEK MEDIATION WHEN NEEDED

Sometimes, conflicts require the involvement of a neutral third party to facilitate resolution. This could be a pastor, elder, or trusted mediator who can provide guidance and perspective. Proverbs 11:14 states, *"Where no counsel is, the people fall: but in the multitude of counsellors there is safety."*

Qualities of an Effective Mediator:

Spiritually mature and grounded in scripture.

Neutral and unbiased in their approach.

Committed to seeking God's will for the situation.

7. FOCUS ON RECONCILIATION AND RESTORATION

The ultimate goal of conflict resolution is reconciliation and restoration, reflecting the heart of God. 2 Corinthians 5:18-19 declares, *"And all things are of God, who hath reconciled us to himself by Jesus Christ, and hath given to us the ministry of reconciliation; To wit, that God was in Christ, reconciling the world unto himself, not imputing their trespasses unto them; and hath committed unto us the word of reconciliation."*

Reconciliation requires effort, patience, and a willingness to rebuild trust. It is not always immediate, but it is always worth pursuing for the sake of unity and the testimony of the church.

Practical Steps for Promoting Reconciliation:

Encourage both parties to focus on their shared faith and mission.

Celebrate small steps toward healing and unity.

Remind the congregation of their collective responsibility to foster peace and love.

CONCLUSION

Handling conflict biblically is not always easy, but it is essential for the health and unity of the church. By acknowledging conflict, approaching it with humility, and following the biblical process for resolution, we can prevent division and promote reconciliation. As Romans 12:18 exhorts us, *"If it be possible, as much as lieth in you, live peaceably with all men."* Through God's grace and guidance, the church can overcome conflict and continue to reflect His glory to the world.

Chapter 4

HEALING AFTER A SPLIT

Church splits are devastating events that leave wounds in their wake, not just for the congregation but for individuals and families who were once united in worship and purpose. Healing after such a traumatic event requires intentionality, humility, and reliance on God's Word. This chapter explores how churches can move forward after a split, rebuild trust, and restore relationships. Drawing from my pastoral experiences, I will provide practical insights and biblical guidance for this delicate process.

ACKNOWLEDGING THE PAIN

One of the first steps toward healing is acknowledging the pain caused by the split. A church split often leaves people feeling betrayed, disillusioned, and disconnected. Ignoring or downplaying this pain can hinder the healing process.

The Apostle Paul reminds us in Romans 12:15, *"Rejoice with them that do rejoice, and weep with them that weep."* Acknowledging the hurt allows individuals to feel seen and validated, which is an essential step toward recovery.

Practical Ways to Acknowledge Pain:

Hold a special service of lament and prayer where members can express their grief and seek God's comfort.

Provide opportunities for members to share their experiences and feelings in a safe and respectful environment.

Offer counseling or pastoral care to those deeply affected by the split.

REBUILDING TRUST

Trust is often one of the first casualties of a church split. Rebuilding it takes time, consistency, and intentional actions. Proverbs 3:5-6 reminds us, *"Trust in the Lord with all thine heart; and lean not unto thine own understanding. In all thy ways acknowledge him, and he shall direct thy paths."* Trust among members begins with trust in God's plan for restoration.

Steps to Rebuild Trust:

1. **Transparency in Leadership:**

   Share decisions openly and explain the reasoning behind them.

   Avoid secrecy, which can breed suspicion.

2. **Consistency in Actions:**

   Follow through on commitments.

   Demonstrate integrity in both small and significant matters.

3. **Fostering Accountability:**

   Create structures where leaders and members are accountable to one another.

   Encourage open communication and feedback.

PROMOTING FORGIVENESS AND RECONCILIATION

Forgiveness is a cornerstone of the Christian faith and a vital component of healing. Ephesians 4:32 commands us, *"And be ye kind one to another, tenderhearted, forgiving one another, even as God for Christ's sake hath forgiven you."* Reconciliation is not always immediate, but it must be pursued diligently.

Steps Toward Forgiveness and Reconciliation:

Teach on Forgiveness: Use sermons, Bible studies, and workshops to emphasize the biblical mandate for forgiveness.

Create Opportunities for Dialogue: Facilitate conversations where members can express their feelings and seek understanding.

Celebrate Small Reconciliations: Highlight stories of forgiveness within the congregation to inspire others.

WHEN HEALING DOES NOT OCCUR

In some cases, healing does not occur after a split. This was my experience at Prince of Peace Baptist Church in Peoria, Illinois. The group I pastored had left another church, and while we worked hard to foster communication and reconciliation, the wounds from the split were too deep for some. Members carried the pain of unresolved conflicts, and attempts to bridge the gap with those who had left were met with resistance. This reality taught me that, while we are called to pursue peace, not all efforts will lead to visible results.

Romans 12:18 reminds us, *"If it be possible, as much as lieth in you, live peaceably with all men."*

HEALING THROUGH WORSHIP AND PRAYER

Worship and prayer play a powerful role in the healing process. They refocus the congregation's attention on God and remind members of their shared purpose.

Psalm 34:18 assures us, *"The Lord is nigh unto them that are of a broken heart; and saveth such as be of a contrite spirit."* Worshiping together fosters unity and reminds the church of God's presence and faithfulness.

Ideas for Worship and Prayer:

Organize prayer vigils focused on healing and unity.

Incorporate songs and scriptures that emphasize reconciliation and restoration.

Encourage members to pray for one another, even for those who left during the split.

REBUILDING RELATIONSHIPS

A church split often fractures relationships, leaving members hesitant to trust or engage deeply with one another. Intentional efforts are needed to rebuild these bonds.

Strategies for Rebuilding Relationships:

1. **Fellowship Opportunities:**

   Host events that allow members to reconnect in informal settings, such as potlucks, picnics, or game nights.

2. **Small Group Ministries:**

   Create small groups that foster deeper connections through shared Bible study and prayer.

3. **Service Projects:**

   Encourage members to serve together in outreach efforts, fostering unity through a shared mission.

MOVING FORWARD WITH A RENEWED VISION

After a church split, it is crucial to refocus on the mission and vision of the church. This provides a sense of purpose and direction for the congregation.

Proverbs 29:18 states, *"Where there is no vision, the people perish: but he that keepeth the law, happy is he."* A renewed vision helps the church move beyond the pain of the past and look toward the future.

Steps to Renew the Church's Vision:

Revisit the church's mission statement and core values.

Involve members in discussions about the church's goals and priorities.

Set achievable short-term and long-term objectives that align with the church's purpose.

DRAWING FROM MY EXPERIENCE

At New Cornerstone Baptist Church, which I had the privilege of organizing, we focused on building a culture of unity from the outset. We emphasized discipleship and fellowship, creating opportunities for members to grow spiritually and relationally. These experiences taught me that healing requires both spiritual and practical efforts, rooted in God's Word and empowered by His grace. However, my journey at Prince of Peace was a sobering reminder that not every effort will lead to full restoration. Sometimes, the best we can do is pray, remain faithful, and trust God with the outcome.

CONCLUSION

Healing after a church split is a challenging but necessary process. It requires acknowledging the pain, rebuilding trust, fostering forgiveness, and refocusing on the church's mission. As Philippians 3:13-14 encourages us, *"Forgetting those things which are behind, and reaching forth unto those things which are before, I press toward the mark for the prize of the high calling of God in Christ Jesus."* By relying on God's guidance and working together, churches can overcome the wounds of division and emerge stronger, united in their purpose to glorify God.

Chapter 5

THE ROLE OF LEADERSHIP

Leadership is one of the most critical factors in determining how a church navigates conflict and division. A leader's approach can either exacerbate tensions or foster healing and unity. This chapter explores the biblical role of leadership during times of division and the qualities necessary for leaders to guide their congregations effectively through challenges. Drawing from my own experiences, I will highlight the lessons I've learned about servant leadership, accountability, and reliance on God.

LEADERSHIP IN THE MIDST OF DIVISION

The Bible is filled with examples of leaders who faced division within God's people. Moses dealt with rebellion among the Israelites, Paul addressed divisions in the early church, and Jesus himself faced opposition from those he came to save. Each of these leaders provides valuable lessons on how to navigate conflict while maintaining integrity and faithfulness.

Proverbs 29:2 reminds us, *"When the righteous are in authority, the people rejoice: but when the wicked beareth rule, the people mourn."* Leadership sets the tone for how a church responds to challenges. A leader's humility, wisdom, and commitment to God's Word are essential for guiding the congregation through difficult times.

1. THE CALL TO SERVANT LEADERSHIP

Jesus set the ultimate example of servant leadership, stating in Mark 10:45, *"For even the Son of man came not to be ministered unto, but to minister, and to give his life a ransom for many."* A servant leader prioritizes the needs of the congregation over personal ambition or gain.

Qualities of a Servant Leader:

Humility: Philippians 2:3-4 instructs, *"Let nothing be done through strife or vainglory; but in lowliness of mind let each esteem other better than themselves. Look not every man on his own things, but every man also on the things of others."*

Empathy: Understanding the pain and struggles of the congregation fosters trust and connection.

Accountability: A servant leader is open to feedback and willing to admit mistakes.

2. LEADING BY EXAMPLE

A leader's actions speak louder than words. In times of division, members will look to their leaders for guidance and reassurance. Paul encouraged Timothy in 1 Timothy 4:12, *"Let no man despise thy youth; but be thou an example of the believers, in word, in conversation, in charity, in spirit, in faith, in purity."*

Ways to Lead by Example:

Model Unity: Demonstrate a commitment to reconciliation and collaboration.

Practice Forgiveness: Show a willingness to forgive and seek forgiveness when necessary.

Maintain Integrity: Uphold biblical principles in decision-making and interactions.

3. ADDRESSING CONFLICT WITH COURAGE AND WISDOM

One of the most challenging aspects of leadership is addressing conflict directly. Avoiding issues often allows them to grow, leading to greater division. Proverbs 15:1 advises, *"A soft answer turneth away wrath: but grievous words stir up anger."* Effective leaders approach conflict with both courage and wisdom.

Steps for Addressing Conflict:

1. **Pray for Guidance:** Seek God's wisdom before taking action.

2. **Gather the Facts:** Ensure you have a clear understanding of the situation.

3. **Engage in Honest Conversations:** Speak the truth in love (Ephesians 4:15).

4. **Seek Reconciliation:** Strive to restore relationships and promote unity.

4. EMPOWERING OTHERS TO LEAD

Leadership is not a one-person role. Effective leaders empower others to step into leadership roles, creating a team that can address challenges collectively. Moses' father-in-law, Jethro, advised him in Exodus 18:21 to appoint capable men to share the burden of leadership, saying, *"Thou shalt provide out of all the people able men, such as fear God, men of truth, hating covetousness; and place such over them, to be rulers of thousands, and rulers of hundreds, and rulers of fifties, and rulers of tens."*

Benefits of Empowering Others:

Reduces the burden on a single leader.

Encourages diverse perspectives and solutions.

Strengthens the overall leadership structure of the church.

5. RELYING ON GOD FOR STRENGTH

Leadership, especially during times of division, can be physically, emotionally, and spiritually draining. Isaiah 40:31 offers encouragement: *"But they that wait upon the Lord shall renew their strength; they shall mount up with wings as eagles; they shall run, and not be weary; and they shall walk, and not faint."* Leaders must prioritize their own spiritual health to effectively guide others.

Practices for Spiritual Renewal:

Spend time in personal prayer and Bible study.

Seek support and counsel from trusted mentors or fellow pastors.

Take intentional breaks to rest and recharge.

6. BUILDING UNITY THROUGH LEADERSHIP

Effective leaders prioritize unity as a central goal for their congregations. Psalm 133:1 declares, *"Behold, how good and how pleasant it is for brethren to dwell together in unity!"* Unity is not achieved by accident; it requires intentional effort and leadership.

Strategies for Building Unity:

Focus on Shared Goals: Emphasize the mission and vision of the church to unite members around a common purpose.

Encourage Collaboration: Create opportunities for members to work together on projects and ministries.

Resolve Disagreements Quickly: Address conflicts before they escalate, fostering a culture of reconciliation.

DRAWING FROM MY EXPERIENCE

In my 35 years of pastoral ministry, I have learned the importance of servant leadership, particularly during times of division. At Southside First Baptist Church in Kansas City, Missouri, I inherited a congregation that had experienced significant turmoil. My focus was on loving the people and restoring order, as Paul instructed Titus in Titus 1:5, *"For this cause left I thee in Crete, that thou shouldest set in order the things that are wanting, and ordain elders in every city, as I had appointed thee."*

At Prince of Peace Baptist Church in Peoria, Illinois, I faced the challenges of leading a group that had left another church. While the pain of the split lingered, I worked to foster open communication and create a vision for the future. Organizing New Cornerstone Baptist Church taught me the value of building a foundation on unity and shared purpose from the outset.

These experiences reinforced the importance of humility, patience, and reliance on God in leadership. They also reminded me that leadership is a stewardship, requiring faithfulness to God and His people.

CONCLUSION

The role of leadership in the church is both a privilege and a responsibility. Leaders have the power to influence the trajectory of their congregations, especially during times of conflict and division. By embracing servant leadership, addressing conflict with courage, empowering others, and relying on God for strength, leaders can guide their churches toward healing and unity.

As Hebrews 13:17 exhorts, *"Obey them that have the rule over you, and submit yourselves: for they watch for your souls, as they that must give account, that they may do it with joy, and not with grief: for that is unprofitable for you."* Faithful leadership brings joy and peace to the church, reflecting the love and grace of Christ.

Leadership is not just about managing challenges but about inspiring a congregation to reflect the unity and love of Christ. It requires humility, courage, and an unwavering commitment to God's Word. Through faithful leadership, the church can overcome division and become a powerful witness of God's grace to the world.

Chapter 6

PREVENTING CHURCH SPLITS BEFORE THEY HAPPEN

The best way to address church splits is to prevent them from occurring in the first place. Prevention requires proactive leadership, biblical teaching, and a commitment to fostering unity within the body of Christ. In this chapter, we will explore strategies for identifying potential sources of division and cultivating a church culture that prioritizes reconciliation, open communication, and spiritual maturity. Drawing from scripture and my pastoral experiences, I will provide practical steps for building a healthy and unified congregation.

THE IMPORTANCE OF PROACTIVE PREVENTION

Church splits often begin with small issues that grow over time due to neglect or mishandling. The Apostle Paul warned the church in Corinth about the dangers of division, saying, *"Now I beseech you, brethren, by the name of our Lord Jesus Christ, that ye all speak the same thing, and that there be no divisions among you; but that ye be perfectly joined together in the same mind and in the same judgment"* (1 Corinthians 1:10). This admonition reminds us that unity is both a command and a collective responsibility.

Preventing division requires vigilance, intentionality, and a reliance on biblical principles to guide the church in every aspect of its ministry.

1. CULTIVATING A SPIRIT OF UNITY

Unity does not happen by accident; it must be nurtured and maintained. Psalm 133:1 declares, *"Behold, how good and how pleasant it is for brethren to dwell together in unity!"* A unified church reflects the character of Christ and serves as a powerful witness to the world.

Practical Ways to Cultivate Unity:

Teach on the Importance of Unity: Regularly preach and teach on passages that emphasize the value of unity, such as John 17:21 and Ephesians 4:3.

Encourage Fellowship: Create opportunities for members to build relationships through small groups, social events, and ministry teams.

Model Unity in Leadership: Ensure that the leadership team demonstrates mutual respect, cooperation, and alignment with the church's mission.

2. ADDRESSING ISSUES EARLY

Small disagreements, if left unaddressed, can escalate into larger conflicts. Leaders must be attentive to potential sources of division and address them promptly.

Steps for Addressing Issues Early:

1. **Listen Actively:** Pay attention to concerns raised by members and take them seriously.

2. **Seek Input:** Involve key leaders or mediators to gain perspective and find solutions.

3. **Take Action:** Implement changes or interventions to resolve the issue before it grows.

Jesus provides a blueprint for addressing conflict in Matthew 18:15-17, beginning with private conversations and escalating to involve others if necessary. This process emphasizes the importance of addressing problems directly and biblically.

3. PROMOTING HEALTHY COMMUNICATION

Miscommunication and gossip are often at the root of division. Ephesians 4:29 advises, *"Let no corrupt communication proceed out of your mouth, but that which is good to the use of edifying, that it may minister grace unto the hearers."*Encouraging open, honest, and respectful communication helps prevent misunderstandings and builds trust.

Practical Tips for Healthy Communication:

Establish clear channels for sharing information within the church.

Encourage members to speak directly to one another rather than spreading rumors.

Provide training on effective communication, including listening skills and conflict resolution.

4. STRENGTHENING SPIRITUAL MATURITY

Spiritual immaturity often leads to division, as members prioritize personal preferences over biblical principles. Hebrews 5:12-14 highlights the importance of growing in spiritual maturity, saying, *"For every one that useth milk is unskilful in the word of righteousness: for he is a babe. But strong meat belongeth to them that are of full age."*

Ways to Strengthen Spiritual Maturity:

Discipleship Programs: Offer Bible studies, mentoring, and classes to deepen members' understanding of scripture.

Prayer Initiatives: Foster a culture of prayer that encourages dependence on God.

Encourage Accountability: Create small groups where members can support and challenge one another in their faith.

5. BUILDING A STRONG LEADERSHIP TEAM

A united and spiritually mature leadership team sets the tone for the entire congregation. Leaders must model humility, integrity, and a commitment to unity.

Qualities of a Strong Leadership Team:

Servanthood: Following Jesus' example in Mark 10:45, leaders should prioritize serving others over seeking power.

Transparency: Open communication among leaders fosters trust and collaboration.

Diversity: A diverse leadership team brings a range of perspectives and strengths, enhancing decision-making and problem-solving.

6. ENCOURAGING RECONCILIATION AND FORGIVENESS

Even in a healthy church, conflicts will arise. Promoting a culture of reconciliation and forgiveness helps prevent these conflicts from leading to division. Colossians 3:13 teaches, *"Forbearing one another, and forgiving one another, if any man have a quarrel against any: even as Christ forgave you, so also do ye."*

Steps to Encourage Reconciliation:

Provide teaching on biblical forgiveness and reconciliation.

Offer mediation or counseling for members experiencing conflict.

Celebrate stories of reconciliation within the congregation to inspire others.

DRAWING FROM MY EXPERIENCE

In my years of ministry, I have seen both the blessings of unity and the devastation of division. At New Cornerstone Baptist Church, we placed a strong emphasis on building a culture of openness, prayer, and collaboration from the beginning. This proactive approach helped us address challenges before they could take root and ensured that our focus remained on Christ and His mission.

At Prince of Peace Baptist Church, the pain of a previous split underscored the importance of addressing issues early and fostering an environment of transparency and trust. These experiences taught me that prevention is far more effective than trying to heal after division has occurred.

CONCLUSION

Preventing church splits requires intentional effort, grounded in scripture and supported by practical strategies. By cultivating unity, addressing issues early, promoting healthy communication, and strengthening spiritual maturity, churches can create an environment where division is less likely to occur.

As Paul wrote in Philippians 2:2, *"Fulfil ye my joy, that ye be likeminded, having the same love, being of one accord, of one mind."* Unity glorifies God and reflects His love to the world. By committing to prevention, leaders and congregations can build strong, thriving churches that stand as beacons of hope and reconciliation.

Chapter 7

RESTORING BROKEN RELATIONSHIPS

Church splits often leave behind a trail of broken relationships—friends and families divided, trust shattered, and fellowship fractured. The process of restoring these relationships requires intentional effort, humility, and a commitment to the principles found in God's Word. In this chapter, we will explore practical steps and biblical foundations for rebuilding trust and fostering reconciliation within the body of Christ. Drawing from my own experiences, I will share how churches can take active steps toward healing.

THE BIBLICAL MANDATE FOR RECONCILIATION

Reconciliation is not just a suggestion; it is a command from God. Jesus taught the importance of reconciliation in Matthew 5:23-24: *"Therefore if thou bring thy gift to the altar, and there rememberest that thy brother hath ought against thee; Leave there thy gift before the altar, and go thy way; first be reconciled to thy brother, and then come and offer thy gift.*" This passage underscores the priority God places on mending broken relationships.

Paul reinforces this mandate in 2 Corinthians 5:18-19, stating, *"And all things are of God, who hath reconciled us to himself by Jesus Christ, and hath given to us the ministry of reconciliation; To wit, that God was in Christ, reconciling the world unto himself, not imputing their trespasses unto them; and hath committed unto us the word of reconciliation.*" As believers, we are called to reflect God's reconciling work in our relationships with one another.

1. ACKNOWLEDGING THE HURT

Before reconciliation can occur, it is essential to acknowledge the hurt caused by the division. Ignoring or minimizing the pain only prolongs the healing process.

Practical Steps to Acknowledge Hurt:

Create Safe Spaces for Dialogue: Provide opportunities for members to express their feelings without fear of judgment.

Listen Actively: Show empathy and understanding by truly listening to others' experiences.

Validate the Pain: Acknowledge the reality of the hurt and its impact on individuals and the congregation.

As Proverbs 18:13 reminds us, *"He that answereth a matter before he heareth it, it is folly and shame unto him."* Listening is the first step toward understanding and healing.

2. EXTENDING FORGIVENESS

Forgiveness is the cornerstone of restoring broken relationships. It is a decision to release bitterness and resentment, even if the offending party has not apologized. Colossians 3:13 instructs, *"Forbearing one another, and forgiving one another, if any man have a quarrel against any: even as Christ forgave you, so also do ye."*

Steps to Foster Forgiveness:

Teach on Biblical Forgiveness: Use sermons and Bible studies to emphasize the necessity of forgiveness.

Pray for a Forgiving Heart: Encourage members to seek God's help in letting go of anger and bitterness.

Celebrate Acts of Forgiveness: Highlight examples of forgiveness within the congregation to inspire others.

3. REBUILDING TRUST

Trust is often one of the first casualties of a church split, and rebuilding it requires time, consistency, and intentional effort. Proverbs 3:5-6 reminds us, *"Trust in the Lord with all thine heart; and lean not unto thine own understanding. In all thy ways acknowledge him, and he shall direct thy paths."* Trust among members must be rooted in trust in God.

Steps to Rebuild Trust:

Be Transparent: Leaders should communicate openly about decisions and initiatives.

Follow Through on Commitments: Consistency in actions fosters credibility.

Encourage Accountability: Establish systems where members can support and hold one another accountable.

4. FACILITATING RECONCILIATION

Reconciliation often requires deliberate action. Matthew 18:15-17 provides a clear framework for addressing conflicts within the church:

1. **Address the Issue Privately:** *"Go and tell him his fault between thee and him alone."* Begin with one-on-one conversations to resolve misunderstandings.

2. **Involve Witnesses:** *"Take with thee one or two more, that in the mouth of two or three witnesses every word may be established."* Bring in neutral parties to mediate if needed.

3. **Seek Church-Wide Support:** *"Tell it unto the church."* Involve the broader congregation as a last resort to encourage resolution.

5. PROMOTING FELLOWSHIP

Fellowship plays a vital role in restoring relationships. Acts 2:42 describes the early church's commitment to fellowship, stating, *"And they continued stedfastly in the apostles' doctrine and fellowship, and in breaking of bread, and in prayers."* Sharing life together helps rebuild connections and fosters a sense of belonging.

Ideas for Promoting Fellowship:

Host Church-Wide Events: Plan activities that encourage members to interact and build relationships.

Encourage Small Groups: Create opportunities for deeper connections through Bible studies or prayer groups.

Serve Together: Organize service projects that unite members around a common goal.

6. HEALING THROUGH WORSHIP AND PRAYER

Worship and prayer are powerful tools for healing broken relationships. They redirect the congregation's focus to God and remind members of their shared identity in Christ.

Incorporating Worship and Prayer:

Plan Special Services of Reconciliation: Dedicate a time for corporate prayer and worship centered on healing.

Use Scripture in Worship: Highlight passages that emphasize unity and forgiveness, such as Ephesians 4:3.

Encourage Personal Prayer: Challenge members to pray for those with whom they have conflicts.

DRAWING FROM MY EXPERIENCE

At Southside First Baptist Church in Kansas City, Missouri, I witnessed the difficulty of restoring broken relationships after a split. The pain was palpable, and the road to healing was long. My role was to encourage open communication, model forgiveness, and point the congregation to God's promises of restoration.

At Prince of Peace Baptist Church, the process of reconciliation was even more challenging. The deep wounds from the split created barriers that were difficult to overcome. These experiences taught me that while reconciliation is always worth pursuing, it is not always immediately achievable. However, trusting in God's timing and continuing to promote unity and forgiveness are vital steps forward.

CONCLUSION

Restoring broken relationships after a church split is a difficult but necessary process. By acknowledging the hurt, extending forgiveness, rebuilding trust, facilitating reconciliation, and fostering fellowship, churches can move toward healing and unity. As Philippians 2:3-4 encourages us, *"Let nothing be done through strife or vainglory; but in lowliness of mind let each esteem other better than themselves. Look not every man on his own things, but every man also on the things of others."*

Through God's grace and the faithful efforts of His people, even the most broken relationships can be restored, reflecting the reconciling love of Christ to a watching world.

Chapter 8

EMBRACING A
NEW BEGINNING

A church split often feels like the end of something precious, but it can also mark the beginning of a new chapter in the life of a congregation. Embracing a new beginning requires faith, resilience, and a willingness to trust God's plan for restoration and growth. In this chapter, we will explore how churches and their leaders can move forward after a split, rebuild their identity, and seize opportunities for renewal. Drawing from my personal experiences and biblical principles, I will outline practical steps for embracing a fresh start.

TRUSTING GOD'S SOVEREIGNTY

The aftermath of a church split can be filled with uncertainty and doubt, but the Bible reminds us that God is sovereign over all circumstances. Romans 8:28 assures us, *"And we know that all things work together for good to them that love God, to them who are the called according to his purpose."* Even in the midst of pain and loss, God is working to bring about His purpose for His people.

Ways to Trust God's Sovereignty:

Reflect on God's faithfulness in the past and trust that He will continue to guide the church.

Commit the future of the congregation to prayer, seeking His wisdom and direction.

Encourage members to hold onto hope and focus on the opportunities ahead.

REBUILDING THE CHURCH'S IDENTITY

After a split, it is essential to redefine and reestablish the church's identity. This process involves revisiting the mission, vision, and core values that define the congregation.

Steps to Rebuild the Church's Identity:

1. **Revisit the Mission Statement:**

   Reflect on the church's purpose and ensure it aligns with biblical principles.

Involve members in reaffirming or redefining the mission to foster unity.

2. **Clarify Core Values:**

   Identify the values that will guide the church moving forward, such as discipleship, community, or outreach.

3. **Cast a Vision for the Future:**

   Outline specific goals and initiatives that reflect the church's renewed identity and mission.

Proverbs 29:18 reminds us, *"Where there is no vision, the people perish: but he that keepeth the law, happy is he."* A clear vision inspires and unites the congregation around a shared purpose.

FOSTERING UNITY IN THE CONGREGATION

Unity is both a gift from God and a responsibility of His people. Ephesians 4:3 exhorts us to be *"endeavouring to keep the unity of the Spirit in the bond of peace."* Cultivating unity after a split requires intentional effort to heal divisions and build trust.

Strategies for Fostering Unity:

Encourage Open Communication: Create safe spaces for members to share their thoughts and concerns.

Promote Fellowship: Organize events and activities that bring members together and strengthen relationships.

Emphasize Common Goals: Focus on shared mission and values to unite the congregation.

SEIZING OPPORTUNITIES FOR RENEWAL

A split can serve as a catalyst for renewal, providing an opportunity to address past challenges and implement positive changes. Isaiah 43:19 declares, *"Behold, I will do a new thing; now it shall spring forth; shall ye not know it? I will even make a way in the wilderness, and rivers in the desert."* God can bring new life and purpose to a church that embraces His leading.

Opportunities for Renewal:

1. **Evaluate Ministries:** Assess the effectiveness of current ministries and identify areas for improvement.

2. **Develop New Leaders:** Invest in leadership development to equip members for service and ministry.

3. **Strengthen Discipleship:** Focus on spiritual growth and maturity through Bible studies, mentoring, and prayer initiatives.

EMBRACING CHANGE WITH FAITH

Change is often difficult, especially after a traumatic event like a church split. However, embracing change with faith allows the church to grow and adapt to new opportunities.

Tips for Embracing Change:

Communicate Clearly: Keep the congregation informed about changes and involve them in the process.

Remain Flexible: Be open to new ideas and approaches that align with the church's mission.

Celebrate Progress: Acknowledge and celebrate milestones along the journey of renewal.

DRAWING FROM MY EXPERIENCE

At New Cornerstone Baptist Church, we faced the challenge of building a new identity after its formation following a split. From the outset, we focused on creating a culture of unity, discipleship, and community engagement. We revisited our mission and vision, involving members in the process to ensure a sense of ownership and commitment. This collaborative approach helped us move forward with clarity and purpose.

At Prince of Peace Baptist Church, I saw firsthand how difficult it can be to navigate the aftermath of a split. While the wounds were deep and the journey was challenging, I learned the importance of relying on God's sovereignty and seeking His guidance in every decision. These experiences taught me that embracing a new beginning requires both faith and action.

CONCLUSION

Embracing a new beginning after a church split is not an easy task, but it is an opportunity for growth, renewal, and restoration. By trusting God's sovereignty, rebuilding the church's identity, fostering unity, and seizing opportunities for renewal, congregations can move forward with hope and purpose. As Philippians

3:13-14 encourages us, *"Forgetting those things which are behind, and reaching forth unto those things which are before, I press toward the mark for the prize of the high calling of God in Christ Jesus."*

Through faith, perseverance, and a commitment to God's Word, churches can rise from the challenges of division and embrace a future filled with promise and possibility.

Chapter 9

THE POWER OF RECONCILIATION

As painful as church splits can be, they also present an opportunity for God's transformative power to work in the hearts of individuals and congregations. Reconciliation—the restoration of broken relationships—is central to the message of the gospel. This chapter explores how reconciliation can be pursued even after deep divisions and highlights the biblical principles and practical steps needed to bring healing to fractured communities. Drawing from scripture and my pastoral experiences, I will share how the power of reconciliation can bring glory to God and renewal to His church.

THE BIBLICAL FOUNDATION OF RECONCILIATION

Reconciliation is at the heart of God's plan for humanity. Through Jesus Christ, God reconciled us to Himself, making peace possible between sinful humanity and a holy God. Paul writes in 2 Corinthians 5:18-19, *"And all things are of God, who hath reconciled us to himself by Jesus Christ, and hath given to us the ministry of reconciliation; To wit, that God was in Christ, reconciling the world unto himself, not imputing their trespasses unto them; and hath committed unto us the word of reconciliation."*

As recipients of God's grace, we are called to extend that same grace to others. Reconciliation within the church reflects God's character and demonstrates the power of the gospel to restore what is broken.

1. RECOGNIZING THE NEED FOR RECONCILIATION

The first step toward reconciliation is acknowledging the divisions and hurts that exist. Pretending that everything is fine only prolongs the pain and prevents healing.

Signs That Reconciliation Is Needed:

Lingering bitterness or resentment among members.

Avoidance of certain individuals or groups within the congregation.

A lack of trust or cooperation in ministry efforts.

Psalm 34:14 instructs, *"Depart from evil, and do good; seek peace, and pursue it."* Seeking peace requires an honest assessment of the barriers to unity.

2. THE ROLE OF HUMILITY IN RECONCILIATION

Reconciliation requires humility from all parties involved. Pride often prevents people from admitting their mistakes or seeking forgiveness. Philippians 2:3-4 reminds us, *"Let nothing be done through strife or vainglory; but in lowliness of mind let each esteem other better than themselves. Look not every man on his own things, but every man also on the things of others."*

Steps to Foster Humility:

Encourage self-reflection and acknowledgment of personal contributions to the conflict.

Emphasize the importance of prioritizing relationships over personal pride.

Model humility as a leader by admitting mistakes and seeking forgiveness when necessary.

3. THE PROCESS OF SEEKING FORGIVENESS

Forgiveness is a critical component of reconciliation. Without it, wounds remain open, and divisions deepen. Jesus taught about the importance of forgiveness in Matthew 6:14-15: *"For if ye forgive men their trespasses, your heavenly Father will also forgive you: But if ye forgive not men their trespasses, neither will your Father forgive your trespasses."*

Steps to Seek and Offer Forgiveness:

1. **Acknowledge the Hurt:** Clearly identify the actions or words that caused pain.

2. **Express Genuine Regret:** Apologize sincerely, without making excuses or shifting blame.

3. **Commit to Change:** Demonstrate a willingness to make amends and avoid repeating the offense.

4. **Release Bitterness:** Choose to let go of resentment and trust God to bring justice.

4. FACILITATING CONVERSATIONS FOR HEALING

Open and honest conversations are essential for reconciliation. These dialogues provide an opportunity for individuals to express their feelings, clarify misunderstandings, and work toward mutual understanding.

Guidelines for Productive Conversations:

Create a Safe Environment: Ensure that all parties feel respected and heard.

Use Neutral Mediators: Involve a trusted leader or counselor to guide the discussion.

Focus on Solutions: Keep the conversation constructive and forward-looking.

James 1:19 advises, *"Wherefore, my beloved brethren, let every man be swift to hear, slow to speak, slow to wrath."* Active listening is a key skill in fostering reconciliation.

5. REBUILDING TRUST OVER TIME

Trust is often the most fragile element in a fractured relationship, and rebuilding it requires time and consistent effort. Proverbs 3:5-6 reminds us to trust in the Lord, who provides the strength and guidance needed for this process.

Steps to Rebuild Trust:

Be Transparent: Keep communication open and honest.

Follow Through on Commitments: Demonstrate reliability in both small and large matters.

Celebrate Progress: Acknowledge and appreciate steps toward reconciliation, no matter how small.

6. THE ROLE OF WORSHIP AND PRAYER IN RECONCILIATION

Worship and prayer are powerful tools for healing and unity. They refocus the church on God and remind members of their shared identity in Christ.

Incorporating Worship and Prayer:

Organize Special Services: Dedicate time for corporate prayer and worship centered on reconciliation.

Encourage Personal Prayer: Challenge members to pray for those with whom they have conflicts.

Use Worship to Promote Unity: Incorporate songs and scriptures that emphasize forgiveness and restoration.

DRAWING FROM MY EXPERIENCE

In my years of ministry, I have witnessed both the challenges and the triumphs of reconciliation. At Southside First Baptist Church, I saw the healing that can occur when members commit to listening to one another and seeking God's guidance. However, at Prince of Peace Baptist Church, the wounds from the split were deep, and reconciliation was a long and difficult process. These experiences taught me that while reconciliation is not always quick or easy, it is always worth pursuing.

At New Cornerstone Baptist Church, we made reconciliation a foundational value from the start. By fostering open communication and emphasizing the importance of unity, we were able to address conflicts early and maintain a spirit of harmony within the congregation.

CONCLUSION

Reconciliation is a powerful testimony of God's grace and love. It requires humility, forgiveness, and a commitment to restoring broken relationships. As Colossians 3:13-14 encourages us, *"Forbearing one another, and forgiving one another, if any man have a quarrel against any: even as Christ forgave you, so also do ye. And above all these things put on charity, which is the bond of perfectness."*

Through God's power, churches can overcome even the deepest divisions and emerge stronger and more unified. Reconciliation is not just a goal; it is a reflection of the gospel and a witness to the transformative power of God's love.

Chapter 10

MOVING FORWARD WITH HOPE

A church split can leave congregations feeling broken and uncertain about the future, but it also presents an opportunity for a renewed commitment to God's mission and a focus on hope. Moving forward after a split requires faith, resilience, and a unified vision for the future. This chapter explores how churches can embrace hope, rebuild their foundation, and continue to serve as the body of Christ. Drawing from scripture and my pastoral experiences, I will provide practical steps and spiritual encouragement for moving forward.

THE IMPORTANCE OF HOPE

Hope is a powerful force that sustains believers through difficult times. Romans 15:13 declares, *"Now the God of hope fill you with all joy and peace in believing, that ye may abound in hope, through the power of the Holy*

Ghost." Even in the aftermath of a split, hope in God's faithfulness can inspire a congregation to press forward.

Biblical Foundations for Hope:

God's Sovereignty: Trusting that God is in control, even when circumstances seem chaotic (Isaiah 41:10).

Christ's Victory: Remembering that Christ has overcome the world (John 16:33).

The Holy Spirit's Guidance: Relying on the Spirit to provide wisdom and strength (John 14:26).

1. REBUILDING THE CHURCH'S FOUNDATION

A church's foundation must be firmly rooted in Christ and His Word. After a split, it is crucial to revisit the core principles that guide the congregation.

Steps to Rebuild the Foundation:

1. **Reaffirm the Church's Mission:**

   Reflect on the church's purpose and ensure it aligns with biblical teachings.

Engage the congregation in discussions about their shared mission.

2. **Prioritize Spiritual Growth:**

Focus on discipleship programs and Bible studies to strengthen the faith of members.

Encourage personal devotion and prayer as foundational practices.

3. **Commit to Sound Doctrine:**

Teach and uphold the truths of scripture, avoiding divisive or speculative topics.

1 Corinthians 3:11 reminds us, *"For other foundation can no man lay than that is laid, which is Jesus Christ."* Building on Christ ensures stability and purpose.

2. CASTING A RENEWED VISION

Vision provides direction and inspiration for the future. Proverbs 29:18 states, *"Where there is no vision, the people perish."* A renewed vision helps the church focus on its mission and energizes members to work together.

Developing a Renewed Vision:

Seek God's Guidance: Pray for wisdom and clarity in setting the direction for the church.

Involve the Congregation: Encourage members to share their ideas and participate in shaping the vision.

Set Measurable Goals: Establish clear objectives that align with the church's mission and values.

3. FOSTERING HEALING AND UNITY

Healing and unity are essential for moving forward. Ephesians 4:3 urges believers to be *"endeavouring to keep the unity of the Spirit in the bond of peace."* Churches must intentionally create an environment where members feel valued and connected.

Practical Steps for Fostering Unity:

Host Reconciliation Events: Plan services or gatherings focused on healing and forgiveness.

Encourage Teamwork: Involve members in joint projects or ministries to build relationships.

Celebrate Diversity: Embrace the unique gifts and perspectives each member brings to the church.

4. EMBRACING OPPORTUNITIES FOR GROWTH

A church split can provide a fresh perspective on ministry opportunities. Isaiah 43:19 reminds us, *"Behold, I will do a new thing; now it shall spring forth; shall ye not know it? I will even make a way in the wilderness, and rivers in the desert."* God often uses challenging situations to open doors for growth and renewal.

Opportunities for Growth:

Strengthening Outreach: Focus on serving the community and sharing the gospel.

Developing Leaders: Invest in leadership training to equip members for ministry roles.

Expanding Ministries: Explore new areas of ministry that align with the church's mission.

5. PERSEVERING THROUGH CHALLENGES

Moving forward is not without obstacles, but perseverance is key. Galatians 6:9 encourages us, *"And* let us not be weary in well doing: for in due season we shall reap, if we faint not." Churches must remain steadfast in their commitment to God's work.

Strategies for Perseverance:

Stay Focused on Christ: Keep the gospel at the center of all activities and decisions.

Encourage One Another: Foster a culture of mutual support and encouragement.

Celebrate Milestones: Acknowledge progress and victories, no matter how small.

DRAWING FROM MY EXPERIENCE

At New Cornerstone Baptist Church, embracing a new beginning was a central part of our journey. After the church's formation, we focused on building a strong foundation rooted in discipleship, prayer, and outreach. By casting a clear vision and involving members in the process, we created a sense of ownership and unity that propelled us forward.

At Southside First Baptist Church, the journey of moving forward required healing and reconciliation. The congregation's willingness to trust God and embrace new opportunities played a significant role in our progress. These experiences taught me that hope and perseverance are essential for navigating the challenges of a new beginning.

CONCLUSION

Moving forward after a church split is a challenging but rewarding process. By rebuilding the foundation, casting a renewed vision, fostering unity, and embracing opportunities for growth, churches can emerge stronger and more focused on God's mission. As Philippians 1:6 assures us, *"Being confident of this very thing, that he which hath begun a good work in you will perform it until the day of Jesus Christ."*

Through faith, perseverance, and a commitment to God's Word, churches can overcome past divisions and step into a future filled with hope and promise. The journey may be difficult, but the rewards of faithfulness and unity are eternal.

Chapter 11

THE FINAL WORD

As this book comes to a close, it is my prayer that the insights, scriptures, and personal experiences shared here will inspire healing, understanding, and unity within the church. Church splits are painful, but they do not have to define the story of God's people. Instead, they can serve as moments of growth, reflection, and renewal when approached with faith and a commitment to reconciliation.

REFLECTING ON THE JOURNEY

Throughout this book, we have explored the causes of church splits, the pain they leave behind, and the paths toward healing and unity. Each chapter has emphasized the importance of humility, forgiveness, and reliance on God's Word as the foundation for addressing division.

Dr. Mark A. McConnell

As I reflect on my own experiences as a pastor in churches that experienced splits, I am reminded of the Apostle Paul's words in 2 Corinthians 4:8-9: *"We are troubled on every side, yet not distressed; we are perplexed, but not in despair; Persecuted, but not forsaken; cast down, but not destroyed."* These words encapsulate the resilience and hope that the church must hold onto, even in the most challenging times.

LOOKING AHEAD WITH HOPE

While the pain of a split can feel overwhelming, it is important to remember that God is a God of restoration. He takes what is broken and makes it whole again. Isaiah 61:3 speaks of giving *"beauty for ashes, the oil of joy for mourning, the garment of praise for the spirit of heaviness."* This promise reminds us that God can bring renewal and revival even from the ashes of division.

Key Takeaways for Moving Forward:

1. **Prioritize Unity:** Commit to fostering a culture of love, respect, and understanding within the church.

2. **Embrace Reconciliation:** Actively seek to mend relationships and build bridges where divisions have occurred.

3. **Focus on Christ:** Keep the gospel at the center of every decision and action, ensuring that the church remains a beacon of hope and light.

A PERSONAL NOTE OF ENCOURAGEMENT

To my fellow pastors, leaders, and church members who may be walking through the aftermath of a split, know that you are not alone. God sees your pain, your struggles, and your efforts to bring healing to His people. Galatians 6:9 encourages us, *"And let us not be weary in well doing: for in due season we shall reap, if we faint not."* Your labor is not in vain, and God will honor your faithfulness.

A CLOSING PRAYER

Heavenly Father,

We come before You with hearts open to Your guidance and grace. You are the God of reconciliation, the One who heals wounds and restores what has been broken. We ask that You bring healing to churches that have experienced division. Help leaders to walk in humility and wisdom, and give congregations the strength to pursue unity and peace. May Your Word be a lamp unto our feet and a light unto our path as we move forward in faith. Let Your name be glorified in all that we do, and may Your church stand as a testimony of Your love and power. In Jesus' name, we pray. Amen.

CONCLUSION

The church is not perfect, but it is God's chosen instrument for spreading the gospel and advancing His kingdom. Through challenges, conflicts, and even splits, the church has the opportunity to demonstrate the transformative power of God's love. By embracing humility, forgiveness, and a commitment to unity, we can reflect the heart of Christ to a world in desperate need of His grace.

As you close this book, may you be reminded of the words of Ephesians 3:20-21: *"Now unto him that is able to do exceeding abundantly above all that we ask or think, according to the power that worketh in us, Unto him be glory in the church by Christ Jesus throughout all ages, world without end. Amen."* Let us move forward together, trusting in God's faithfulness and committed to His purpose.

ABOUT THE AUTHOR

Dr. Mark A. McConnell was born on February 7, 1963, and raised in Kansas City, Kansas, by devoted Christian parents. From a young age, his faith was central to his life, accepting Christ at the tender age of five. Dr. McConnell's foundational spiritual upbringing was nurtured at Mt. Zion Baptist Church under the guidance of Dr. C.L. Bachus.

He pursued higher education with a commitment to his calling, earning a Bachelor's degree in Religion and Philosophy from Bishop College in Dallas, Texas, in 1986. He continued his theological education, receiving a Master of Divinity from Midwestern Baptist Theological Seminary in Kansas City, Missouri, in 1989 and completing a Doctor of Theology (Th.D.) in May 2002.

Dr. McConnell has been blessed with a beautiful family. He married Paris McConnell, his steadfast partner and source of strength, on September 2, 1989. Together, they have three sons—Moses, Caleb, and Matthew—and are proud grandparents to Jayden and Jordan McConnell.

Answering the call to preach, Dr. McConnell delivered his first sermon in May 1984 and was ordained in August 1985. His pastoral journey has included leading three congregations: Southside First Baptist Church in Kansas City, Missouri; Prince of Peace Baptist Church in Peoria, Illinois; and currently, New Cornerstone Baptist Church in Peoria, Illinois. His service extends beyond the pulpit, having served two terms as Moderator of the Central Illinois Baptist District Association in Peoria, Illinois. His involvement with the Baptist General State Convention of Illinois spans over 31 years, during which he has held significant positions, including 2nd Vice President of both the Baptist General Congress of Christian Education and the Baptist General State Convention of Illinois.

Dr. McConnell's dedication and unwavering commitment have led to his current role as President of the Baptist General State Convention of Illinois. His passion for this esteemed body is evident in his consistent participation, having never missed a board meeting, annual session, or Congress of Christian Education. He firmly believes that God has positioned him to lead and serve, fostering unity and growth within the convention.

Dr. McConnell's vision is clear: to uphold and advance the legacy of the Baptist General State Convention of Illinois, continuing its history as a leading force among state conventions. Through dedication and collective effort, he is confident that this convention will remain a beacon of leadership, faith, and service.

Printed in the United States
by Baker & Taylor Publisher Services